ideals®
EASTER
2006

Dedicated to a celebration of the American ideals of faith in God, loyalty to country, and love of family.

Features

Departments

Cover: Rain-kissed tulips dance in a garden in Skagit Valley, Washington. Photograph by Terry Donnelly/Donnelly Austin Photography.

Inside front cover: How welcome are the soft yellows of early spring, as represented in this painting by Mary Kay Krell, entitled JONQUILS AND LACE. Photograph by Steve Beasley.

IDEALS—Vol. 63, No. 1, January 2006 IDEALS (ISSN 0019-137X, USPS 256-240) is published six times a year: January, March, May, July, September, and November by Ideals Publications, 39 Seminary Hill Road, Carmel, NY 10512. Copyright © 2006 by Ideals Publications. All rights reserved. The cover and entire contents of IDEALS are fully protected by copyright and must not be reproduced in any manner whatsoever. Title IDEALS registered U.S. Patent Office. Printed and bound in the USA. Printed on Weyerhauser Husky. The paper used in this publication meets the minimum requirements of American National Standard for Information Sciences—Permanence of Paper for Printed Materials, ANSI Z39.48-1984. Periodicals postage paid at Carmel, New York, and additional mailing offices. Canadian mailed under Publications Mail Agreement Number 40010140. POSTMASTER: Send address changes to IDEALS, 39 Seminary Hill Road, Carmel, NY 10512. CANADA POST: Send address changes to Guideposts, PO Box 1051, Fort Erie ON L2A 6C7. For subscription or customer service questions, contact Ideals Publications, 39 Seminary Hill Road, Carmel, NY 10512. Fax 845-228-2115. Reader Preference Service: We occasionally make our mailing lists available to other companies whose products or services might interest you. If you prefer not to be included, please write to Ideals Publications Customer Service.

ISBN 0-8249-1306-X GST 893989236

Visit our website at
www.idealspublications.com

The Prophecy

Patience Strong

Only a green tip sharp and small, but a fresh hope it has brought. A dream of spring in a cold, gray world, a new and daring thought. Only a speck in the frosted grass, but it means that all is well. Soon a flower on a slender stalk will ring a fairy bell. Just a snowdrop by the way—lighting up the wintry day.

Only the point of a thrusting leaf, but it promises so much—breaking the iron of the frozen earth with a light and magic touch. Only a rumor, a secret hint, a whispered prophecy, thrilling my heart with the promised joy of the golden days to be. Only a tiny, tender thing—but it hails the distant spring.

*Pink magnolia blossoms float over the snow in
Hidden Lake Gardens, Lenawee County, Michigan.
Photograph by Darryl R. Beers.*

Flurries

Dathene Stanley

I walked along the winding road,
Admiring spring's wondrous rebirth,
When suddenly the snow began
To fall in flurries full of mirth.
The air soon filled with gentle snow,
Which gathered on each hill and bank
And finely dusted each hedgerow.
Large flakes surrounded snowdrops too;
They even powdered grass new-green;
They veiled the yellow daffodils;
The world was now a fairy scene.
A moment only snow did fall,
But lines and angles it erased;
The world was innocent again,
That lovely moment born in grace.

One Flower's Merit

Ralph W. Seager

I do esteem the summer rose,
And let no one deride my choice,
For what would a wedding or birthday be
Without such a beauty to rouse my voice?
Still, when I come to think on it,
The rose sure has it made of all
The best that buds could ever wish:
Those sunny days, summer till fall.

Then I look back to the small crocus bloom,
One that has only a brief week to show
Valor while wearing the purple and gold—
And does it standing alone in the snow.
No other metaphor can focus
So well on courage as the crocus.

Petite crocus blooms peer above the snow in this garden in Corvallis, Oregon. Photograph by Dennis Frates.

COUNTRY CHRONICLE

Lansing Christman

SPRING SNOW

Easter snows come as no surprise, whether Easter comes in the latter hours of March or in those rich April days of tender sprouts, swelling buds, and bursting blooms.

When a spring snow sweeps in to slow the thaw, to blanket roof and slope and wall, the finery is a delicate pattern with bright spots of color that hint at the rainbow of new growth and new life to come. Robins and redwings and cardinals, crossbills and redpolls and purple finches—all blend their reds, purples, and pinks with the rich, rusty hue of the fox sparrow, the yellows of the goldfinch and the grosbeak, and the white of snow.

Even more beautiful are the songs that accompany the last snowfall: the robin carols and the redwing flutes, the liquid warble of the bluebird and fox sparrow songs. Lovely melodies and delightful trills fill the days as winter paints its last self-portrait.

And spring is born once more in a clinging snow of soft and feathered flakes, born again in song in a season when men pause to bow in celebration of resurrection and new life.

The author of four books, Lansing Christman has contributed to IDEALS for more than thirty years. Mr. Christman has also been published in several American, international, and braille anthologies. He lives in rural South Carolina.

Purple Gem rhododendrons and early tulips announce the arrival of spring. Photograph by Larry LeFever/Grant Heilman.

Waiting for Spring
Laurie Dawson Wilcox

I waited for spring upon a high hill,
To catch the first note of the sad whippoorwill,
To watch the wild geese in orderly flight
Dip in the horizon and then out of sight.

I waited for spring upon a creek bank
And floated leaf boats until they all sank;
I flew my new kite into the blue sky
And laughed as it rose like a gay butterfly.

I waited for spring while searching for flowers
And wandered so deep into the wood bowers;
There, violets were waiting to carpet a room,
And redbud was ready to burst into bloom.

I waited for spring almost everywhere;
I knew it was soon, for its breath filled the air;
And one morning I woke and heard my heart say,
"I waited for spring and this is the day."

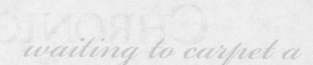

There, violets were waiting to carpet a room, And redbud was ready to burst into bloom.

Spring: Sing!
Eileen Spinelli

The robin chirps,
the crocus blooms,
the scent of green
spills through old rooms.
Oh, we have known
these things before—
the breeze against
the back screen door,
the golden sun,
the sky of blue
again . . . again . . .
yet somehow new.
The grass grows tall,
spring hums along—
our hearts
can scarcely hold
the song.

Above: A pink, large-flowered trillium is one of the forest's treasures in Shenandoah National Park, Virginia. Photograph by Terry Donnelly/Donnelly Austin Photography.

Redwood sorrels and flowering trilliums decorate the forest floor in the Green Valley Creek area of Vashon Island, Washington. Photograph by Mary Liz Austin/Donnelly Austin Photography.

Spring Valley

Ruth B. Field

Come, follow the road
That winds through the dale
And over the hills
In their mantles of green,
Past laughter of water
In silvery veil,
Down aisles of birch
With satin-white sheen.
The valley of springtime
With beauty now fills,
The cherry-tree mist
And apple-lace bloom;
A small village nestles
By meadows and hills;
And old dreams awake
In dusk's fragrant bloom.

Go wander where memories
Drift through time's bars,
Where echoes of laughter
Return from lost time—
Spring valley, where music
Is written in stars
And the heart will remember
Life's young, lilting rhyme.

*Spring has come again.
The earth is like a child who knows poems.*
—Rainer Maria Rilke

*Rows of lavender curve through a field on Vashon Island, Washington.
Photograph by Terry Donnelly/Donnelly Austin Photography.*

HOMETOWN AMERICA

Brenda Wilt

CELINA, TENNESSEE

When I think of my hometown, included in almost every memory is the sparkle of light on water. Celina is nestled in the Eastern Highland Rim, a patchwork of beautiful, forested hills and deep hollows between Knoxville, to the east, and Nashville, in the center of the state. Nine miles from the Kentucky border and three miles from Dale Hollow Lake, Celina has natural boundaries formed by two important rivers.

The town is located at River Mile 380, on the south bank of the Cumberland River, at its junction with the Obey. Those rivers have provided material for stories for many generations—stories of Davy Crockett, riverboat pilots, and even Civil War battles. But many afternoons, my sister, Barb, and I created our own stories in the canebrakes by the Cumberland, forging trails through the thick undergrowth.

As a child, I took for granted the fact that East Lake Avenue led directly to the river. My father told me that in low-lying areas people used to tie their boats to the top of their front porches in case of floods, which occurred frequently. I learned to drive on the bottomland roads, and I took each of my daughters there for her first driving experience.

The bridge spanning the Cumberland leads directly to the town square. The most impressive building downtown is the old courthouse, built in 1873 of bricks made from clay taken from the site. I remember retired men gathered on the benches in front when the weather was warm, talking and whittling small sticks of cedar.

Also in town was the law office of Cordell Hull, Secretary of State for President Franklin Roosevelt; in 1945, he was awarded the Nobel Peace Prize. My parents often discussed his life as an inspirational example for my sister and me. The small wooden structure was recently moved to the grounds of the Clay County Museum, for preservation.

As a child, I took for granted the fact that East Lake Avenue led directly to the river.

Each August, Celina hosts Homecoming Days. For a week, people are entertained by old-time fiddlers and other musicians as they walk by booths overflowing with homemade jams, jellies, and large, sugar-dusted pies. Craftsmen of all types offer their wares; my favorites were the basket weavers who gave demonstrations of their skills. Sometimes my sister and I would pause to watch games of marbles known as "Rolley Hole," played by two-man teams on

Dale Hollow Lake. Photograph courtesy of State of Tennessee Tourist Development.

small fields cleared of grass. They competed in matches that required shooting their marbles in a complicated progression into three separate, carefully aligned holes. In the evening we ambled home, tired but pleasantly full of good memories.

Another special occasion that brought the town together was Easter Sunday. In early spring, my sister and I watched Mother sew new dresses for us to wear. When the weather was chilly, she would also make us light coats that we called dusters. She polished our patent leather shoes with a leftover biscuit till they shined. After church, families headed to the park next to Dale Hollow Lake for the annual Easter egg hunt; since my father was one of eighteen children, we had many cousins join us.

Dale Hollow Lake was created in 1943 by the dam built on the Obey. The lake covers more than twenty-six thousand acres, including the towns of Willow Grove and Lily Dale, which were evacuated and intentionally flooded as part of the dam project. My sister and I would watch scuba divers exploring the submerged towns, visible through the clear, clean water.

In winter, the surface of Dale Hollow Lake is marked by tones of deep blue; in spring and summer, its surface is broken by the white collars of boat wakes. My family spent many long, hot days at the lake on my aunt and uncle's boat, swimming and fishing. In the late afternoon, we would sit on the deck of the boat and savor the taste of fried catfish, which we had caught, cleaned, and battered in corn meal. Small green fishing boats dotted the lake, and the distant putter of their motors was background for our leisurely conversations.

Today, although I live many hours from Celina, I cannot see the shimmer of the sun on water without thinking of Dale Hollow Lake. I cannot hear the rush of the Cumberland River without feeling the desire to revisit the small town of my childhood, a place where freedom was bare toes burrowed in warm mud on the riverbank or the cool splash of water accompanied by a friend's laughter—a place where we all felt safe and loved.

Spring

Henry Wadsworth Longfellow

In all climates spring is beautiful. In the South it is intoxicating and sets a poet beside himself. The birds begin to sing; they utter a few rapturous notes and then wait for an answer in the silent woods. Those green-coated musicians, the frogs, make holiday in the neighboring marshes. They, too, belong to the orchestra of Nature, whose vast theater is again opened, though the doors have been so long bolted with icicles, and the scenery hung with snow and frost, like cobwebs. This is the prelude which announces the rising of the broad green curtain.

The white blossoms of the cherry hang upon the boughs like snowflakes.

Already the grass shoots forth. The waters leap with thrilling pulse through the veins of the earth; the sap through the veins of the plants and trees; and the blood through the veins of man. What a thrill of delight in springtime!

What a joy in being and moving! Men are at work in gardens; and in the air there is an odor of the fresh earth. The leaf-buds begin to swell and blush. The white blossoms of the cherry hang upon the boughs like snowflakes; and ere long our next-door neighbors will be completely hidden from us by the dense green foliage. The Mayflowers open their soft blue eyes.

Children are let loose in the fields and gardens. They hold buttercups under each others' chins to see if they love butter. And the little girls adorn themselves with chains and curls of dandelions; pull out the yellow leaves to see if the schoolboy loves them; and blow the down from the leafless stalk to find out if their mothers want them at home.

And at night so cloudless and so still! Not a voice of living thing, not a whisper of leaf or waving bough, not a breath of wind, not a sound upon the earth nor in the air! And overhead bends the blue sky, dewy and soft, and radiant with innumerable stars, like the inverted bell of some blue flower sprinkled with golden dust and breathing fragrance. Or if the heavens are overcast, it is no wild storm of wind and rain but clouds that melt and fall in showers. One does not wish to sleep, but lies awake to hear the pleasant sound of the dropping rain.

Above: Cherry blossoms are miniature masterpieces of nature. Photograph by Darryl R. Beers.

White cherry blossoms rise toward a brilliant blue sky in this orchard near Egg Harbor, in Door County, Wisconsin. Photograph by Darryl R. Beers.

Spring

April

Edgar A. Guest

April, and the showers are falling;
April, and the birds are calling
To their kin of song and feather,
Quite regardless of the weather.

From the ground the cold is going;
Now the violets are showing,
And the constant pitter-patter
Of the rain seems not to matter.

April, and the birds are humming
Everywhere that May is coming;
Plant and tree are not complaining
That this morning it is raining.

All around us there is beauty,
Smiling, faithful to its duty;
And the dandelion humble
Seems too big and brave to grumble.

When it's April in our dreaming
And the storms of care are teeming,
May we see beyond our sorrow
All the beauty of tomorrow.

Spring rain touches the faces of a cluster of daffodils.
Photograph by William H. Johnson.

FOR THE CHILDREN

Today It's Raining

Eileen Spinelli

Today it's raining.
I don't mind;
this rain's the
gentle-falling kind,
the kind that puddles
playfully—
"Come out and splash!"
it calls to me—
the kind of rain
that greens the trees
and paints the grass
and cools the breeze;
a rain whose drops
become a song
inviting me to hum along;
a happy rain
called "April showers,"
where bright umbrellas
bloom like flowers.

Artwork by Russ Flint.

April Rain

Mildred L. Evenson

We ran and splashed, my child and I,
In swirling puddles running by.
She laughed and wrinkled up her nose
At Mother squishing with her toes;
And all the earth was fresh and green,
And not a neighbor could be seen.
It was such fun that new spring day
When early April skies gave way,
And no one near or passing by—
Just April rain, my child, and I.

Inspiration

Beth LaPointe Heath

I hear you knocking, pretty rain,
Softly at my windowpane;
For spring has come this April noon,
Tossing sweet, melodious tunes.
Votive nature again shall rise
To echo songs in playful surprise,
While I in joy must lightly go
To plant tomatoes, row on row.

Above: The petals of a single salmon-and-yellow tulip are washed by dewdrops.
Photograph by Terry Donnelly/Donnelly Austin Photography.

A tulip garden filled with a rainbow of blooms brightens a weathered split-rail fence in Skagit County, Washington.
Photograph by Terry Donnelly/Donnelly Austin Photography.

First Plowing

Ralph W. Seager

His farmer-uncle told him he could plow
The furrow that would open up the field;
Although he was unsure that he knew how,
The man within him squirmed to be revealed.
One horse, one plow, one boy, stood there together;
Adventure's thrill ran hot within his veins.
Yoked to each other by the harness tether,
He spoke "Giddap" and slapped the leather reins.
The point bit deep; the sod rolled off the share.
He gripped the wooden handles, knuckles tense,
To keep himself in line with plow and mare
And lay the furrow straight. They reached the fence.
    He turned. And there along the after-view,
    He saw that he had split the world in two.

Spring Labor

Marie J. Post

How blessed are all who plant their fields
To feed their hungry fellow men,
Who plow and sow long hours, long days
And look ahead to autumn when
Their toil has multiplied for them
The ripe, full ear and golden wheat
That hungry people everywhere
May have enough to eat.
Their names are linked with God's,
Who sow their fields with loving care.
Their eyes stay heavenward
In trusting love and thankful prayer.

We ask Thee, Lord, to bless their work,
Send down Thy rain, Thy sun,
That no child anywhere may want
When harvest time is done.

Crabapple blossoms frame this barn in Kewaunee County, Wisconsin, near Dykesville. Photograph by Ken Dequaine.

Spring on the Farm

Craig E. Sathoff

As fresh as bubbling waterfalls,
Its scent is in the air;
For here and there about the farm,
Spring touches everywhere.

It's in the wobbly-legged colts
That frolic in the grass,
And in the red-winged blackbird's nest
And meadowlarks that pass.

It's in the regal irises
Around the old windmill,
And in the fragrant apple trees
That bloom upon the hill.

It's in the furrows newly turned
And in the sacks of seed.
It's in the pheasant's vibrant call
And newborn calves at feed.

As fresh as bubbling waterfalls,
Its scent is in the air;
For here and there about the farm,
Spring touches everywhere.

Another season is upon the land. The plow
wakes the earth from its slumber and ribbons
the field with rich, black furrows to grasp and
nourish the seed.

Once more I plant and wait, sustained by
a harvest reaped, not from the land, but a quiet
faith born of other seasons, heart-ripened,
soul-stored, and secure.

—ROBERT KING

A Paso Fino mare shelters her twin colts in a spring meadow.
Photograph by Gemma Giannini/Grant Heilman.

SLICE OF LIFE

Edna Jaques

SPRING

The smell of burning maple boughs,
    White seagulls following after plows,
A killdeer piping in the rain—
    We wondered if he'd come again
From the warm southland where he goes
    To get away from winter snows.

The starlings came five hundred strong
    And swooped down with a burst of song
To feed upon a chickweed patch,
    Like happy folk who know the latch
Is ever out for their return;
    For them the candles ever burn.

A man works with his pruning shears;
    We wonder if he ever hears
The choir of song above his vines
    Or the tall wind blowing through the pines,
Where clouds as white as thistledown
    Drift over his fields toward the town.

A tractor putts in from the gate
    To turn brown furrows clean and straight;
A little girl in overalls
    Is playing with a pair of dolls
Under an apple tree nearby,
    Which waves its branches at the sky.

There is a feeling in the air
    Of new life coming everywhere,
In beast and bird and creeping thing;
    Of earth responsive to the spring;
Of joy and beauty gathered here,
    And heaven bending very near.

*The responsibilities of spring are lightened by such a beautiful day
as that depicted in the painting entitled TENDING by Robert Duncan.
Image provided by Robert Duncan Studios.*

Wake-up Time
Eleanor Flock

Springtime is the gardener's time;
He plants his seeds with care.
He never doubts the outcome—
He knows God's hand is there.

Green
Lucile Coleman

I love to plant each tiny seed
In my own small plot of land;
I love the feel of warm, brown earth
Within my hopeful hand.
And when I see the glory grown
From such a tiny thing,
I marvel at the miracle
Of the touch of spring.

Joyful Gardener
D. A. Hoover

Spading in the mellow garden,
Sunshine warmth and glow,
Bright-eyed robin searching near
The even, moist, black row;
Seed can balanced on a fence post,
Cackling hens scratch nearby,
I watch a woolly cloud patch float
In a high and deep blue sky.
Raking, smoothing, dropping kernels,
I my golden dreams have spun;
Bumper harvest, recreation—
Every precious minute fun.

Geraniums and purple violets are part of this lovely home garden.
Photograph by William H. Johnson.

READERS' REFLECTIONS

Springtime
Inge Lawrenz
Gardner, Kansas

A lukewarm breeze in the air,
Folks are just now aware
Winter is over and done;
Grass is showing; the snow is gone.

Tulips begin to slowly show;
It's exciting to watch the flowers grow.
People are ready to plant a garden;
No chance anymore the ground will harden.

Loosen the soil for seeds to be put in;
Vegetables are picked out; let the harvest begin.
Now again it's time to start mowing.
God created the ground for growing.

A Spring Recipe
Sister Beatrice Engle
Lowell, Ohio

A dash of cold, chilly air,
A squeeze of a breeze—
Make a mixture of these.
A sprinkle of rain, sliding
Down a windowpane;
A drop of thawing sod, waiting
For a seed to grow;
All being churned and
Turned from below.
Garnish with a bit
Of fertilizer.
A yellow and green world
Begins to grow.

Spring
Janet R. Sady
Mayport, Pennsylvania

Oak branches stretch knobby limbs
To slip on emerald dresses.
Daffodils turn golden faces
Drinking in sun from the east;
Rose-breasted grosbeaks flutter
And preen before their mates.
Orioles join in the symphony.
Fishermen cast nylon lines at
Trout and catfish who
Lurk beneath shaded rocks.
Feathery seeds float through
The air searching for spots
To lay their heads.
Spring teases with mellow days
And gentle breezes;
New growth springs from barren soil.
While winter melts with new-mown grass
And sun-drenched days,
Spring returns, suitcase in hand,
Ready to move again
When summer knocks.

Life's Awakening
Faye Adams
De Soto, Missouri

The soil lies dormant and still,
Catching snowflakes as they spill
On twigs and branches, piling deep,
Drinking raindrops as they seep,
Anticipating heat from the sun
When winter's work is finally done.

All nature, asleep in winter freeze,
Awakens in the merry March breeze.
Like needles piercing burlap, plants
Toil, pushing upward through the soil,
Strain toward light, battling wind
With joy; let the new cycle begin.

The earth responds in utter delight;
Dull hues change to rainbow brights.
Hang out feeders; fill the birdbath;
Place pansies along the garden path;
Watch the swallows, robins, and jays
Building nests on bright new days.

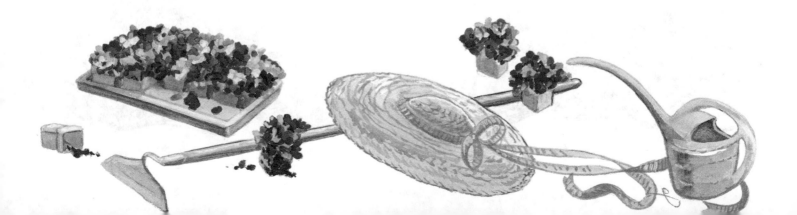

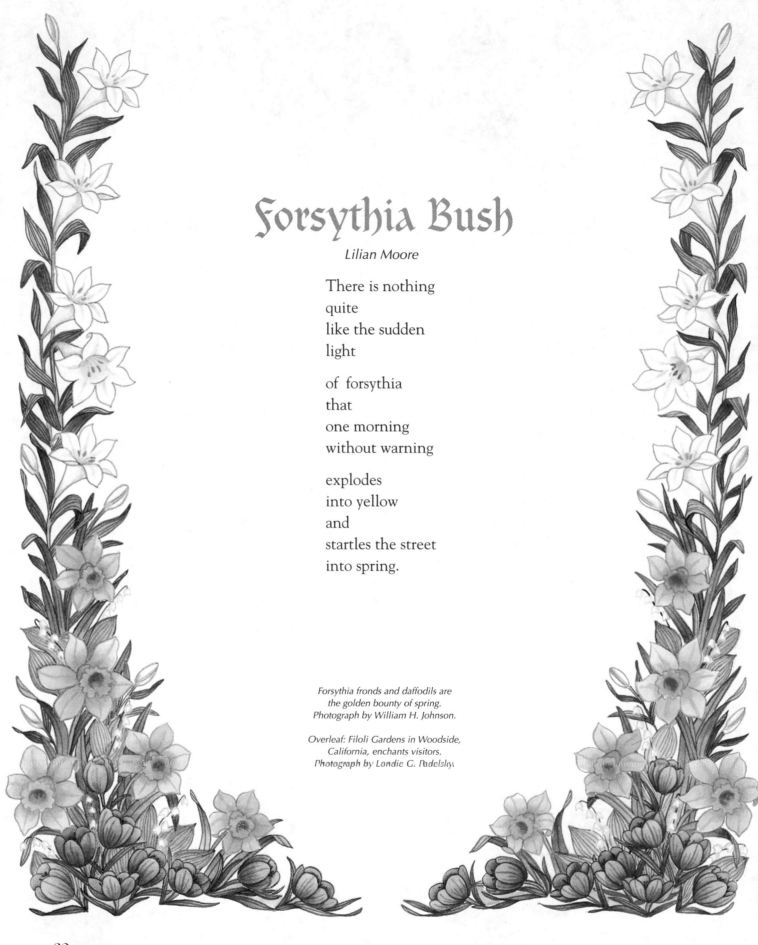

Forsythia Bush

Lilian Moore

There is nothing
quite
like the sudden
light

of forsythia
that
one morning
without warning

explodes
into yellow
and
startles the street
into spring.

*Forsythia fronds and daffodils are
the golden bounty of spring.
Photograph by William H. Johnson.*

*Overleaf: Filoli Gardens in Woodside,
California, enchants visitors.
Photograph by Londie G. Padelsky*

There Will Always Be a Violet

Dorothy Walker

When winter's skies are overcast,
And spring's warm sun peeps through,
What joy to see a violet,
Blessed with morning dew.
A tiny face of beauty fresh,
A message bright with cheer—
A message dropped from heaven
That tells us spring is here.
There'll always be a violet
Along life's dreary way
To bring us hope and promise bright
Of one more sunny day.

Violets

Addie Abele

When I kneel to gather violets,
The long years fade away,
And I am now a child again
On a warm and sunny day,
Walking through a shady lane
Where purple violets grow.
And as I touch their velvet heads,
How am I to know
That every year my heart will ache
With sweet remembering
Of misty dreams and little girls
And violets and spring?

Dandelions insist on taking their place alongside violets in a spring garden.
Photograph by William H. Johnson.

BACKYARD CALENDAR

Joan Donaldson

Ragged cumulus clouds sail from the west, and their shadows glide over my garden. The wooden fence cannot contain the dance of light and dark. One cloud scatters a score of raindrops before it rushes further inland and away from Lake Michigan. I dash to the lee side of my garden shed and wait for the shower to end.

An Irish writer I discovered defined such moments as "bright spells and showers." A smattering of rain rarely halts Irish gardeners, nor will it interrupt my spring afternoon. After all, frustrations can pass through any situation and are like short showers that merely slow us down.

I hug my bag of onion sets to protect them from the sprinkles. Already, white windflowers and violas glisten in the sunlight streaking across the freshly tilled bed. Jewel raindrops sparkle on the cold-frame windows. Beneath the clear plastic sashes, lettuce and chervil stretch towards the sky.

Now that the earth has passed through the vernal equinox and the daylight hours continue to expand, the seeds I planted last November are thriving. Today I can pick a host of fresh greens and, like tasty hors d'oeuvres, the salads will hint at the bounty to come. But I must shoulder my responsibilities of preparing the soil and sowing.

My husband has already raked the soft beds and drawn faint lines where I should plant. He has accepted my inability to draw straight rows.

Left to my own devices, my zinnias would wander, and the paths would grow narrower until we would be stepping on the carrots. So many times in our thirty-year marriage, we have learned to complement each other's weaknesses in order to fulfill our goals.

I slip sassafras sticks at the ends of John's markings to indicate the rows and then deepen the trough with my hoe before plopping the tiny bulbs into the furrows. From the open paper bag a pungent scent fills the air, and I dream of fresh green onions, onion soufflés, and bread dressing speckled with chopped onions.

Five months from now, these onions will add zest to family meals, but those rewards begin now with each golden-skinned globe. My Creator will bring the increase as the earth moves in its determined orbit and sudden showers freshen the soil.

Near the end of the row is a clump of violas that volunteered to brighten that spot. Their yellow and purple faces float amid a tangle of leggy stems and leaves. These hardy flowers are one of the first to bloom; sometimes I find them peeking up after a February thaw.

When I try to rearrange the violas so they will grow away from my onions, something moves. A shallow impression, tucked under the tangle, is lined with gray fur. Three baby rabbits with half-closed eyes and shell-pink ears snuggle closer. I wonder if their mother is the rabbit who invaded my garden this winter and feasted on the

Original artwork by Stacy Venturi-Pickett.

tops of carrots that we left in the ground for a winter treat.

I replace the canopy of leaves and flowers, thinking myself foolish to encourage this family. But I admire the mother rabbit, for she also appreciates having flowers sweeten her home.

Dusting off my hands, I eye the band of gray clouds creeping towards me. I hope I will have enough time to broadcast the compost reserved for the garden. I hoist a five-gallon bucket down the path. As I fling fertilizer across the beds, I can smell rain in the air. The fingers of clouds crawl closer, and I toss faster, knowing that healthy soil yields a successful garden.

A few large raindrops mix with the compost. A shower would soak the fertilizer into the ground, but I would appreciate it even more if I could finish this task first.

As the clouds spread over the sky, I finally yield to the heavens. A cup of tea is more appealing than working in the drizzle, and a mama rabbit needs me to leave so she can protect her offspring.

I race to the house, knowing that tomorrow will offer another afternoon of bright spells and showers spent among seed packets and spring flowers.

Joan Donaldson is the author of books for children and young adults, as well as essays that have appeared in national publications. She and her husband raised their sons on Pleasant Hill Farm in Michigan, where they continue to practice rural skills.

SPRING PROMISE

D. A. Hoover

When spring was new and robins came,
Sun splashed the earth with rainbow flame;
The gardener brought his tools and seeds
To plant and tend and fight the weeds.
By patient toil his crop grew on,
A reward for work from early dawn.
God gave the soil, sent sun and rain;
The lesson He teaches is simple and plain:
Earth's bounty is taken by just one plan—
The partnership of God and man.

MYSTERY

Elsie E. Thornburg

I hold these seeds within my hand,
    Though hard, dry shells they seem to be;
But yet I know, locked tight within,
    They're somehow filled with mystery.

I hold these seeds and something stirs,
    A beauty striving to be free;
But if I now neglect to sow,
    They will forever lifeless be.

So I'll obey the urge to plant,
    Do all that's in my meager power,
And know somehow I've once more helped
    God create a perfect flower.

*This garden cottage is perfect for making plans
for a garden and enjoying the view too.
Photograph by Jessie Walker.*

A Gardener's Song

Mathilde Edna Adams

My heart was singing all the noon;
My spirits soared on high.
The day was crisp and clear and bright
With the sun high in the sky.

My fingers dug the rich, brown earth,
Cool as September rains;
I planted tender cuttings there
Of firm, new-sprouting canes.

In peaceful solitude I felt
My heart grow more in tune
With Him who, from a wee green bark,
Fashions a rose in June.

To cultivate a garden is to walk with God.

—Christian Nestell Bovee

*Flowering dogwoods, tulips, and myriad other spring flowers make
the cottage garden a beautiful setting in this painting by Diane Phelan,
entitled* SPRING GARDEN. *Copyright © Diane Phelan Watercolors.
All rights reserved.*

BITS & PIECES

*F*lowers may beckon toward us, but they speak toward heaven and God.

—*Henry Ward Beecher*

*T*o cultivate the sense of the beautiful is one of the most effectual ways of cultivating an appreciation of the divine goodness.

—*Christian Nestell Bovee*

*C*ame with her trembling banner of perfumed bells The lily of the valley . . .

—*Titus Munson Coan*

*S*peak to the earth, and it shall teach thee.

—*Job 12:8*

There is not the least flower but seems to hold up its head and to look pleasantly, in the secret sense of the goodness of its heavenly Maker.

—Robert South

Truth and goodness and beauty are but different faces of the same All. But beauty in nature is not ultimate. It is the herald of inward and eternal beauty.

—Ralph Waldo Emerson

The heavy Easter lilies . . .
That in our garden grow.

—T. B. Aldrich

But who will watch my lilies,
    When their blossoms open white?
By day the sun shall be sentry,
    And the moon and stars by night!

—Bayard Taylor

45

Cycle of Loveliness
Marion Doyle

Plum blossoms fall in a soft white shower;
They've had their special, shining hour.
Apple blooms will take their place,
All radiant as an angel's face;
And when these beauties have gaily gone
In rosy clouds upon the lawn,
Rambler roses will then appear—
So it goes throughout the year.
Autumn mums bob sunny heads
Over frost-sered garden beds.
And even icy January
Boasts gilt cone and scarlet berry.
Beauty, favorite child of God,
Springs eternal from the sod
Of a garden and survives,
Just as surely, in our lives.

Plum Blossoms
William Arnette Wofford

Who has not loved the cold, wet smell
Of plum trees blooming in the rain,
Or seen a petaled carpet spread
From fallen blossoms in a lane?

Oh, often I have brought them home
In April, branches pearly white,
And placed them in a jade-green bowl
To glow throughout a spring-filled night.

Though I have been away for long,
I still can sense their wild, sweet smell
And hear the drowsy hum of bees
Close to the place I used to dwell.

I, so tired of city streets,
Have need to turn my steps again,
Back to a winding country path
And smell plum blossoms in the rain.

Blossoms from cherry trees spill over into this lane in Edgartown, Martha's Vineyard, Massachusetts. Photograph by Dick Dietrich/Dietrich Leis Stock Photography.

Signs of Spring

Annabelle Stewart Altwater

If all the calendars somehow were lost,
I would know, I would know it is spring;
For even when threatened by late-coming frost,
Undaunted, the woodthrushes sing.
I passed by an old weeping willow when she
Was just donning her new chartreuse bonnet,
All trimmed with ribbons of fine filigree
And a cardinal swinging upon it.
And here between highway and pine-needled shade
Where garrulous mockingbirds call,
The small, wild verbenas have carefully laid
Purple carpet, unseamed, wall-to-wall.
Do not run, little skunk; by that bearded old oak
Is the most tender food of your choice;
Do not be disturbed by the frog's raucous croak
Or the bluejay's loud, fussy voice.
Were there no calendars, were there no dates,
By the daffodils' breath, and a breeze in my hair,
Sun stripes on the grass, birds calling their mates,
I would know there is spring in the air.

Faith

Ona Jane Meens

The seeds stirred by the warmth of sun
Will break their bonds when spring has come,
So slender faith that yearns for light
Can push aside the hampering night
And open up an avenue
That lets the love of God shine through.

48

*A pink dogwood reigns over spring plantings.
Photograph by Larry LeFever/Grant Heilman.*

...would know, I would know it is spring...

Easter Gifts

Mildred L. Jarrell

Lovely are all Easter flowers;
Their perfume's in the air.
They're fresh and sweet from April showers
With colors blended fair.
Lily has a horn-shaped blossom,
The tulip a dainty cup,
The pansy a little pixie face,
And hyacinth's curled up.
The purple crocus peeps above
The violet bed below,
While daffodils in marching drill
Are standing in a row.
Forsythia in yellow dress
Greets spring again so gay,
And pussy willows climb a bush
In softest shades of gray.
Oh, what a lovely gift to bring
As springtime comes our way
And earth abounds with life anew,
This glorious Easter day.

Love's Gift

Craig E. Sathoff

Each daffodil, each cloud above,
And every robin's call
Seem but the motives to enhance
The blessed gift of love—
Easter's hope, our second chance,
Redemption made for all.

*Purple-and-white pansies and pink tulips are a
combination to delight any gardener's hopes.
Photograph by Jessie Walker.*

APRIL SONG

Brian F. King

We give Thee thanks, O Lord, for these:
Soft April rains, green budding trees,
The hush of dawn, gold daffodils,
The songs of birds from sun-kissed hills,
For star-strewn skies whose glory glows
To light the sleeping world below,
For smiling brooks that seek the sea—
We humbly give our thanks to Thee.

We give Thee thanks, O Lord, for these:
The things of life that daily please,
For comfort that is ever there
In hearts that seek Your peace through prayer,
For gardens rich with flowers gay,
For shouts of children lost in play,
The hush of dawn, lakes blue and still,
For daisies strewn on wind-kissed hills.

We give Thee thanks, O Lord, for care
Thy love has lavished everywhere,
For faith and hope, for sacred bliss
That lies in every toddler's kiss,
For bounties shared, for all Thy grace
That blesses every dwelling place,
For dreams unshackled, spirits free—
We give Thee thanks, O Lord, for these.

An attractive table makes breakfast an inviting treat. Photograph by Jessie Walker.

SOMEONE TO REMEMBER

Teresa Schell

A QUIET INFLUENCE

As I brush my hair, I glance at the reflection in my dresser mirror and see my four-year-old son on the bed, comfortably relaxing on his stomach, quietly watching me. I am reminded of another bedroom from my past, with the same dresser.

I am the one lying on my stomach, quietly watching Grandma. It is a Saturday, and she has just finished washing her hip-length hair. She brushes her hair in front of the open window, occasionally smiling at me; when her hair is dry, she plaits it in one long braid that she winds on top of her head. This fond memory reminds me of the influence Grandma continues to have on my life. I learned so much about beauty, generosity, and caring as she quietly went about the daily activities of her life.

My younger sister and I lived close to our grandparents' home, and we visited often. My sister enjoyed following Grandfather around as he tended the vegetable garden, but I preferred staying close to Grandma. She often sat with me when I stayed home from school due to asthma, and her voice soothed me as I rested. The white cotton apron she always wore during the day rubbed my cheeks as she cuddled me in her lap.

In the colder months, Grandma hand-pieced beautiful quilts and crocheted warm afghans to share with family and neighbors. She allowed me to sort small pieces of fabric saved from old clothes and coats, while she sewed and listened to my chatter. Grandma helped me with the Bible verses that I was learning, and one of my earliest memories is her quoting the Twenty-third Psalm.

Nearly every item that Grandma sewed, crocheted, or knitted went to someone else. For each of her thirteen grandchildren Grandma pieced a quilt. My sister and I and our cousins wore mittens, scarves, socks, and slippers made by Grandma. As a teenager, I wanted a then-fashionable open-weave vest to wear to school, and Grandma crocheted more than one for me.

Her home overflowed with laughter and children's voices.

During the late winter, Grandma began to plan her garden. She enjoyed growing flowers, not surprising for a woman whose name was Lorena Viola. As soon as the snows cleared, she would be outside with her gardening tools and collection of seeds she had saved from the previous year's blooms. As my sister and I grew older, Grandma enlisted our help with spreading the seeds.

While outdoors, Grandma would wear old-fashioned calico bonnets to protect her face. Each day in spring, she would walk beside the flowerbeds, murmuring encouragement to the fledgling plants. As the bachelor buttons, poppies, petunias, and pansies began to bloom, she would talk to them as if they were children. "Aren't you beautiful!" she might exclaim to one, and I do believe this actually helped the flowers grow. Some of the flowers were collected into bouquets for the church, but most remained in the flowerbeds.

My favorite flowers were her geraniums, in rich shades of red and pink. When winter approached, Grandma would take geranium cuttings inside the house and keep these flowers blooming even when snow covered the ground. I later realized that she understood we all needed a touch of beauty during the months we had to spend mostly indoors.

Grandma always inspected Grandfather's vegetable garden on her daily excursions, and she explained to my sister and me that the corn, squash, potatoes, green beans, and tomatoes would be cooked and canned for the entire family, and that much would be given to those neighbors who had no gardens.

During the 1930s, neighborhood children would come over to play with my mother and her six siblings. When Grandma called her children in for supper, the friends would follow, and she would feed them too. Her home overflowed with laughter and children's voices. This hospitality continued with her grandchildren and our friends. My friends always wanted to visit with my grandmother when they came to play; the cookies she had waiting for us on the kitchen table would still be warm from the oven.

My memories of Grandma remind me of the virtuous woman described so beautifully in

Vintage hats await the warmth of spring Sundays. Photograph by Dianne Dietrich Leis/Dietrich Leis Stock Photography.

Proverbs: "She seeketh wool, and flax, and worketh willingly with her hands. . . . She sretcheth out her hands to the poor; yea, she reacheth forth her hands to the needy" (31:13, 20). From Grandma, I learned so much that has held true—how to enjoy life's simple tasks, how to make things I need out of what I have, and how to be content with what I have. Grandma demonstrated that generosity is defined not by how much a person has, but by the willingness to share.

Teresa Schell lives with her family in Idaho, where she works with high school students with learning disabilities.

FAMILY RECIPES

CALICO SALAD

Velda Keeney, Rolla, Missouri

1 16-ounce package frozen baby
    lima beans
1 15-ounce can early peas
1 2-ounce jar sliced pimientos
½ cup slivered almonds

½ cup sour cream
¼ cup mayonnaise
¼ teaspoon garlic salt
¼ teaspoon salt
⅛ teaspoon freshly ground pepper

Prepare lima beans according to directions on package; drain well. In a large bowl, combine lima beans, peas, pimientos, and almonds. Set aside. In a medium bowl, combine sour cream, mayonnaise, garlic salt, salt, and pepper. Fold into lima bean mixture. Cover and refrigerate 1 hour or until well chilled. Makes 8 servings.

CREAMY PEA SALAD

Naomi Dyer, Eaton, Colorado

2 16-ounce packages frozen peas,
    thawed
½ cup shredded Cheddar cheese
½ cup shredded mozzarella cheese
1 medium onion, chopped

1 cup mayonnaise
1 teaspoon salt
½ teaspoon pepper
4 bacon slices, cooked and
    crumbled

In a large bowl, combine peas, cheeses, and onion. Stir in mayonnaise, salt, and pepper. Mix well. Refrigerate. Just before serving, sprinkle with bacon. Makes 6 servings.

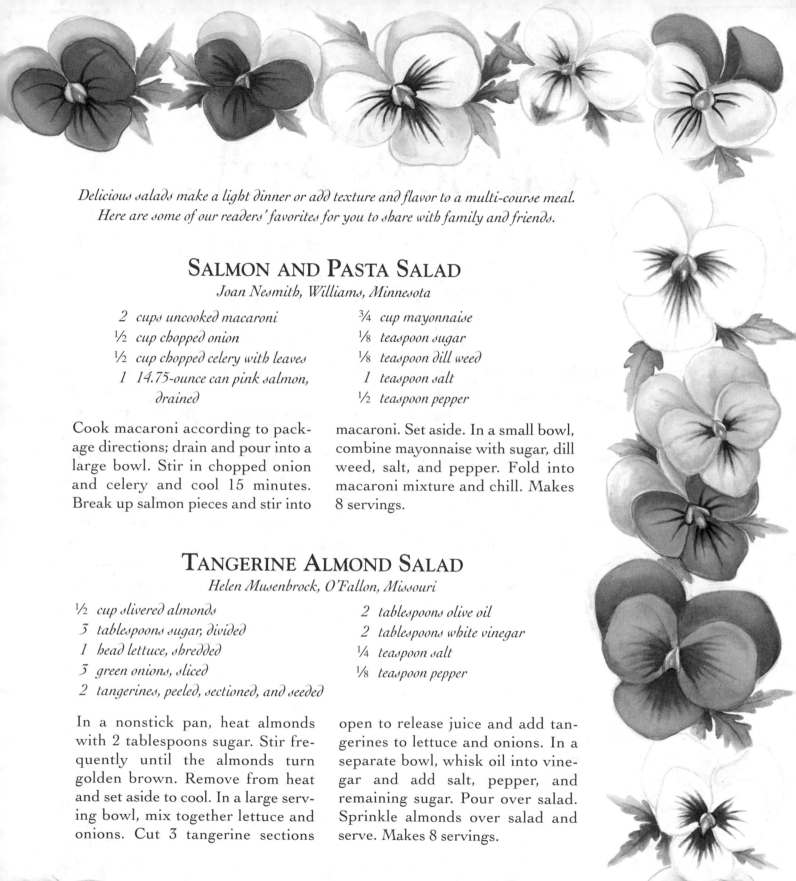

Delicious salads make a light dinner or add texture and flavor to a multi-course meal.
Here are some of our readers' favorites for you to share with family and friends.

SALMON AND PASTA SALAD

Joan Nesmith, Williams, Minnesota

2	cups uncooked macaroni	¾	cup mayonnaise
½	cup chopped onion	⅛	teaspoon sugar
½	cup chopped celery with leaves	⅛	teaspoon dill weed
1	14.75-ounce can pink salmon, drained	1	teaspoon salt
		½	teaspoon pepper

Cook macaroni according to package directions; drain and pour into a large bowl. Stir in chopped onion and celery and cool 15 minutes. Break up salmon pieces and stir into macaroni. Set aside. In a small bowl, combine mayonnaise with sugar, dill weed, salt, and pepper. Fold into macaroni mixture and chill. Makes 8 servings.

TANGERINE ALMOND SALAD

Helen Musenbrock, O'Fallon, Missouri

½	cup slivered almonds	2	tablespoons olive oil
3	tablespoons sugar, divided	2	tablespoons white vinegar
1	head lettuce, shredded	¼	teaspoon salt
3	green onions, sliced	⅛	teaspoon pepper
2	tangerines, peeled, sectioned, and seeded		

In a nonstick pan, heat almonds with 2 tablespoons sugar. Stir frequently until the almonds turn golden brown. Remove from heat and set aside to cool. In a large serving bowl, mix together lettuce and onions. Cut 3 tangerine sections open to release juice and add tangerines to lettuce and onions. In a separate bowl, whisk oil into vinegar and add salt, pepper, and remaining sugar. Pour over salad. Sprinkle almonds over salad and serve. Makes 8 servings.

FROM AMERICA'S ATTIC

Lois Winston

FRILLS, FEATHERS, AND FLOWERS

In your Easter bonnet, with all the frills upon it, / You'll be the grandest lady in the Easter parade." Irving Berlin wrote those memorable words in 1948 for a song in a new Broadway play, later made into a movie entitled *Easter Parade*, starring Fred Astaire and Judy Garland.

The actual Easter Parade began in New York City in the 1870s. As fashionably dressed people arrived at their respective churches and strolled leisurely down Fifth Avenue, onlookers noted and discussed their finery. By the 1880s, the parade was reported in detail in newspapers.

Hats have long been an important social and fashion statement. An indelible image persists in the minds of those who have seen the glamour of Marlene Dietrich's top hat or the elegance of First Lady Jacqueline Kennedy's pillbox atop her bouffant hairdo. The helmet-shaped cloche of the 1920s and '30s, with the brim so low women had to tilt their heads back in order to see, forced women to literally change their stance.

In certain periods of the past, no well-bred lady left the house without a head covering; for many years women kept their heads covered while indoors as well, with white morning caps.

Dependent upon hairstyles, available materials, dress silhouettes, and popular culture, the design of the American woman's hat has had a varied and fascinating history. But the nineteenth and early twentieth century were particularly hat-friendly.

Bonnets in various forms dominated women's fashion for fifty years, beginning in 1810. These bonnets usually had ribbons or velvet strings that tied under the chin, with the sides often hiding the face and the neck from view. Made of straw, board, or silk-covered buckram, bonnets were decorated with ribbons, flowers, feathers, and gauze trims.

The demand for feathers was so great that many birds risked extinction.

By 1860, the parasol had become a fashion staple, reducing the function of a head covering to that of an ornamental accessory. Bonnets became more frivolous. Spoon bonnets, for example, featured peaked crowns decorated with flowers and were perched toward the front of the face, atop the era's large hairstyles.

The trend toward frivolity continued to the point that, by the 1880s, hats were piled high with feathers, fruit, and entire stuffed birds and reptiles. A woman could be decked out in a hat that included egret plumes, owl heads, sparrow wings, and four or five stuffed warblers perched on her head! The demand for feathers was so great that many birds, including the snowy egret and the ostrich, risked extinction.

In 1896, a group of Boston women began boycotting hats decked out with stuffed birds and feathers. Following the example of the editor of *Forest and Stream*, these ladies named their group the Massachusetts Audubon Society. This small movement led to the formation of the national organization in 1905.

The years between 1895 and 1914, called *La Belle Époque*, are known for opulence. Hats became so enormous, with brims as much as four feet in width, that at public performances and the new moving picture theaters a sign was displayed requesting ladies to remove their hats.

The demand for fancy plumage intensified during the early 1900s. The ideal fashion silhouette was an S-curve; and the hat cantilevered over the face or swirled around the head swathed in tulle and was elaborately decorated. Pompadour frames were used underneath hair as an anchor. As the dress silhouette slimmed, the hats widened. The hat's stability increasingly depended upon hatpins. In 1908, an English judge ordered a group of suffragettes to remove their hats in court because he feared that the hatpins, some as long as eighteen inches, could be used as weapons.

With the proliferation of the automobile, the enormous, feather-draped hat became cumbersome. A woman might look elegant with her ostrich plume floating behind her as she rode sidesaddle on her horse, but the effect was not nearly as appealing when she motored along at forty miles an hour.

Then, in 1913, hat design took an abrupt turn. Led by Irene Castle, a popular ballroom dancer, the American woman's preference in hairstyles went from elaborately coifed and complicated curls, buns, and chignons to the bouncing bob. Smaller hats fitted closer to the head. For the more sophisticated, only two long plumes, called Mephisto feathers, pointed upward. For eveningwear, headbands of satin or

A young lady is prepared for a spring outing with her bouquet and lace-draped hat, pictured on this vintage postcard, circa 1915. Photograph by BTH Popperfoto/Retrofile/H. Armstrong Roberts.

velvet, embroidered or trimmed with a feather or two, were worn.

In the decades that followed, Greta Garbo's fedora and Lily Daché's snood were widely copied. Designers continued to promote hats as important accessories. However, with a few exceptions, the hat no longer held the status it once had. Today, except for the occasional queen or princess, head coverings are primarily utilitarian because the modern American woman prefers a casual hairstyle.

But our imaginations can still parade us down The Avenue, when attics give up their frilled, feathery secrets.

Lois Winston is a freelance writer and designer whose work appears regularly in craft and women's magazines. She is also the author of a mystery novel.

Easter Morning

Elsie Natalie Brady

The friendly church across the way
Welcomes all to come inside
And worship on this Easter day.
Its doors, like arms, are open wide;
A scent of flowers fills the air;
Buds have burst; the earth is dressed
In greenery most everywhere.
And on this special day of rest,
The organ swells, and church bells ring
Out the message, loud and clear:
Christ is risen, Christ the King,
To all believers, far and near.

Easter Week

Charles Kingsley

See, the land, her Easter keeping,
    Rises as her Maker rose.
Seeds, so long in darkness sleeping,
    Burst at last from winter snows.
Earth with heaven above rejoices;
    Fields and gardens hail the spring;
Shores and woodlands ring with voices,
    While the wild birds build and sing.

You, to whom your Maker granted
    Powers to those sweet birds unknown,
Use the craft by God implanted;
    Use the reason not your own.
Here, while heaven and earth rejoice,
    Each his Easter tribute bring—
Work of fingers, chant of voices,
    Like the birds who build and sing.

The Easter People

Vangie Roby Sweitzer

"The Lord is risen," the pastor intones. Echoing back from the hundreds assembled comes, "The Lord is risen indeed!"

In towns and cities across America, the dawn of Easter Day awakens Christians to sunrise services. Perhaps nowhere is that service more stirring in its age-old simplicity than in Bethlehem, Pennsylvania.

Just as darkness gives way to the first light of dawn and the chirping of birds is heard, another sound floats over the campus of Central Moravian Church. The mellow voices of trombones echo along Church Street and across the flat gravestones adorned with pink, purple, and white hyacinths. Once again, as they have for more than 250 years, the trombones have led the gathered worshippers from the sanctuary of the Central Moravian Church to God's Acre, an early Moravian cemetery.

Pastors representing the six Bethlehem Area Moravian churches lead the worshippers in word and song as they affirm their faith in the risen Savior.

Of the several hundred who encircle the gravesite, some are visitors from far and wide. Most, however, are members of the city's first congregation, the oldest Moravian church in North America, whose forebears founded Bethlehem in 1741.

One of the oldest Protestant denominations in the world, the Moravian church had its beginnings one hundred years before Martin Luther gained his place in history. In Bohemia, now part of the Czech Republic, a Roman Catholic priest named John Hus attempted to reform the Church. He was declared a heretic and burned at the stake in 1415. His followers from Moravia and Bohemia established a separate church in 1457, which survived two centuries of religious persecution, until they were provided a safe haven on a nobleman's estate in Saxony.

As dawn breaks, the trombonists lead the congregation to God's Acre.

As part of a larger German tradition of using bands of wind instruments for both church and community functions, the Moravians held their first Easter Dawn service in Saxony in April 1732, and a trombone choir was a part of that service.

The church began to send missionaries to various part of the world, including the New World, and along with them went their instruments, as well as hymnals and manuscripts of choral and instrumental music.

In 1755, the first quartet of slide trombones was used for the Easter Dawn service in Bethlehem. The original "set" of instruments, fashioned in Europe and sent to the settlements, included a small soprano trombone, called a "slide trumpet" and extremely rare today; a slightly larger alto trombone in E flat; and the standard tenor and F bass trombones. The Bethlehem choir has since added other trombones, including a 125-year-old F bass trombone almost eight feet long.

Other Moravian settlements also used trombone choirs, and many included several other instruments. However, the only brass instrument of the time capable of playing a chromatic scale in the range of the human voice, the trombone was a natural to accompany church services, to sound chorales from the roof of Bethlehem's Single Brethren's House on special occasions, and to announce the arrival of dignitaries, as had been customary in Europe.

When the Bethlehem Moravians completed the vast sanctuary known as the Central Moravian Church in 1806, the trombone choir began its tradition of playing from the church's massive belfry for special occasions.

Since that time, in a firmly entrenched tradition, the trombonists have gathered each Easter morning. They travel about the city, pausing under street lights to play their chorales outside the homes of selected members and pastors. They then assemble in the choir loft of the church, where they perform the opening chorale of the Easter morning liturgy. As dawn breaks, the trombonists lead the congregation to God's Acre, where the service is concluded.

The congregation disperses to enjoy traditional sugar cake and coffee and to attend the worship service in the Old Chapel. The trombonists slip away, probably to sleep.

Shortly before ten, children gather for an egg

Young boys hold torches to illuminate the music in this engraving of the trombone choir that appeared in Harper's Weekly *March 31, 1888. Image courtesy of Central Moravian Church, a National Landmark of Music.*

hunt on the church green with much competition from the local squirrel population. Each egg has a cache of candy and printed Bible verses.

At eleven, the Easter Triumph service begins, and there is room for more than a thousand worshippers. The chancel area is filled with dozens of palms. A graceful cross of white lilies stands among them.

As the Easter Liturgy begins, members experience both an exhilaration and a peace knowing that they are standing in a place defined by a beloved heritage. These are the "Easter People."

In this bright and beautiful old sanctuary, the Easter Liturgy concludes, and the congregation and the choir rise with anticipation and join in singing the beloved hymn of Resurrection:

Sing hallelujah, praise the Lord!
Sing with a cheerful voice:
Exalt our God with one accord,
And in His name rejoice.

Hosanna

Entry into Jerusalem

Mark 11:1–10

And when they came nigh to Jerusalem, unto Bethphage and Bethany, at the mount of Olives, he sendeth forth two of his disciples,

And saith unto them, Go your way into the village over against you: and as soon as ye be entered into it, ye shall find a colt tied, whereon never man sat; loose him, and bring him.

And if any man say unto you, Why do ye this? say ye that the Lord hath need of him; and straightway he will send him hither.

And they went their way, and found the colt tied by the door without in a place where two ways met; and they loose him.

And certain of them that stood there said unto them, What do ye, loosing the colt?

And they said unto them even as Jesus had commanded: and they let them go.

And they brought the colt to Jesus, and cast their garments on him; and he sat upon him.

And many spread their garments in the way: and others cut down branches off the trees, and strawed them in the way.

And they that went before, and they that followed, cried, saying,

Hosanna; Blessed is he that cometh in the name of the Lord:

Blessed be the kingdom of our father David, that cometh in the name of the Lord:

Hosanna in the highest.

in the highest

CHRIST'S ENTRY INTO JERUSALEM *by Santi di Tito (1536–1603).*
Image from Art Resource, NY/Scala/Accademia, Florence, Italy.

Gethsemane

Matthew 26:36–45

Then cometh Jesus with them unto a place called Gethsemane, and saith unto the disciples, Sit ye here, while I go and pray yonder. And he took with him Peter and the two sons of Zebedee, and began to be sorrowful and very heavy.

Then saith he unto them, My soul is exceeding sorrowful, even unto death: tarry ye here, and watch with me. And he went a little farther, and fell on his face, and prayed, saying, O my Father, if it be possible, let this cup pass from me: nevertheless not as I will, but as thou wilt.

And he cometh unto the disciples, and findeth them asleep, and saith unto Peter, What, could ye not watch with me one hour? Watch and pray, that ye enter not into temptation: the spirit indeed is willing, but the flesh is weak.

He went away again the second time, and prayed, saying, O my Father, if this cup may not pass away from me, except I drink it, thy will be done.

And he came and found them asleep again: for their eyes were heavy. And he left them, and went away again, and prayed the third time, saying the same words.

Then cometh he to his disciples, and saith unto them, Sleep on now, and take your rest: behold, the hour is at hand, and the Son of man is betrayed into the hands of sinners.

the Son of man is betr

CHRIST IN THE GARDEN OF OLIVES *by Eugene Delacroix (1798–1863). Image from Art Resource, NY/Giraudon/St. Paul-St. Louis, Paris, France.*

Crucifixion

Mark 15:20–28

And when they had mocked him, they took off the purple from him, and put his own clothes on him, and led him out to crucify him.

And they compel one Simon a Cyrenian, who passed by, coming out of the country, the father of Alexander and Rufus, to bear his cross.

And they bring him unto the place Golgotha, which is, being interpreted, The place of a skull.

And they gave him to drink wine mingled with myrrh: but he received it not.

And when they had crucified him, they parted his garments, casting lots upon them, what every man should take.

And it was the third hour, and they crucified him.

And the superscription of his accusation was written over, THE KING OF THE JEWS.

And with him they crucify two thieves; the one on his right hand, and the other on his left.

And the scripture was fulfilled, which saith, And he was numbered with the transgressors.

and the scr

CHRIST CARRYING THE CROSS *by Paolo Veronese (1528–1588).*
Image from Art Resource, NY/Giraudon/Louvre, Paris, France.

...pture was fulfilled

he i

Resurrection

Mark 16:1–6

And when the sabbath was past, Mary Magdalene, and Mary the mother of James, and Salome, had bought sweet spices, that they might come and anoint him.

And very early in the morning the first day of the week, they came unto the sepulchre at the rising of the sun.

And they said among themselves, Who shall roll us away the stone from the door of the sepulchre?

And when they looked, they saw that the stone was rolled away: for it was very great.

And entering into the sepulchre, they saw a young man sitting on the right side, clothed in a long white garment; and they were affrighted.

And he saith unto them, Be not affrighted:

Ye seek Jesus of Nazareth, which was crucified: he is risen; he is not here: behold the place where they laid him.

risen; he is not here

THE THREE MARYS AT THE TOMB *by Annibale Carracci (1560–1609).*
Image from Art Resource, NY/Scala/Hermitage, St. Petersburg, Russia.

The Road to Emmaus

Luke 24:13–16, 25–31

And, behold, two of them went that same day to a village called Emmaus, which was from Jerusalem about threescore furlongs. And they talked together of all these things which had happened.

And it came to pass, that, while they communed together and reasoned, Jesus himself drew near, and went with them. But their eyes were holden that they should not know him. . . .

Then he said unto them, O fools, and slow of heart to believe all that the prophets have spoken: Ought not Christ to have suffered these things, and to enter into his glory?

And beginning at Moses and all the prophets, he expounded unto them in all the scriptures the things concerning himself.

And they drew nigh unto the village, whither they went: and he made as though he would have gone further.

But they constrained him, saying, Abide with us: for it is toward evening, and the day is far spent.

And he went in to tarry with them. And it came to pass, as he sat at meat with them, he took bread, and blessed it, and brake, and gave to them.

And their eyes were opened, and they knew him.

and their eyes were ope

SUPPER AT EMMAUS *by Santi di Tito (1536–1603).*
Image from Art Resource, NY/Scala/St. Croce, Florence, Italy.

ed, and they knew him

THROUGH MY WINDOW

Pamela Kennedy

A MOTHER'S PRAYER

Her son had always been difficult. From an early age he rebelled against the smallest correction, turning away from her with an angry retort. Zahara had named her son Daniel, after the ancient prophet, hoping he would be strong in the faith of the Fathers. But his own father had died while he was very young, and Daniel grew up resenting the God whom he felt had stolen his beloved *abba*. By the time he was a teenager, Daniel ran with a group of young boys who terrorized the citizens of Jerusalem, breaking into homes, stealing from the markets, lying in wait in dark alleyways to pounce on drunken revelers heading home in the early morning hours.

Zahara prayed for her son daily, beseeching God to forgive him, to help him see the error of his ways, to lead him to repentance, but so far her prayers had gone unanswered. She offered sacrifices on behalf of Daniel at the temple. But it was as if the smoke from her offerings had been swept away by the wind before it could ascend to the heavens and the Lord.

Lately, Zahara had joined with a group who followed a new rabbi named Jesus. He welcomed both men and women and taught them that God was not only interested in justice, but also in mercy. He said that those who were weary could receive rest for their souls and find peace with God.

Zahara was certainly weary. She was worn out with worry and disappointment. Her only son, who should have been providing for her, hardly had time to visit. And when he did come by their tiny house in the poor neighborhood where she lived, it wasn't to offer help, but to ask for food or money. After his last visit, she had discovered the small leather bag of silver coins she had hidden under an earthen jar was emptied. He hadn't even left her one.

When He spoke these words, Zahara felt like He was looking into her soul.

Jesus said that the poor in spirit were blessed, that mourners would be comforted, and that the meek would inherit the earth. When He spoke these words, Zahara felt like He was looking into her soul. He talked of hope for the hopeless and new life for the dying. That was Daniel, she thought—lost and on a path leading to certain destruction.

And then the rabbi told them to ask and seek in prayer, beseeching God for the blessings they desired. Zahara did. She trusted this good rabbi and followed Him all over Galilee, drinking in His words like a parched desert.

When she received news that Daniel had been arrested and thrown into the Roman prison, she prayed even more fervently. Perhaps at last God would change his heart.

Then, when the day came that she heard her son had received a death sentence, she almost lost hope. The other disciples reminded her that Jesus had said nothing was impossible for God. "Oh, Father in heaven," she cried, "please save my wayward child."

But now there was new turmoil in her heart. Jesus, their beloved rabbi, was arrested as well, convicted on trumped-up charges and sentenced to death. If God could not save this Righteous One from the Roman cross, what hope was there for Daniel?

Zahara mourned and gathered with the other women, climbing the hill behind their beaten Lord. When she thought her grief could be no greater, she raised her eyes to the hillside of Golgotha and gasped.

There, on a cross to the left of Jesus, was Daniel, her son. She fell to her knees and wailed, crying out to God in one final, desperate prayer. Then, it was as if the sounds of the crowd and the weeping women stilled, and Zahara heard men speaking. She raised her eyes slowly to the three crosses silhouetted against the midday sky.

"If You're the Christ, save Yourself and us too!" mocked the man on the right.

Jesus turned His head away and gazed at Daniel. Zahara held her breath as she saw her son look into the eyes she had learned to love and trust. Then Daniel spoke, quietly but with conviction.

"Have you no fear of God? We deserve what we're getting, but this man has done nothing wrong. Oh, Lord, please remember me when You come into Your kingdom."

The voice of her beloved rabbi echoed from the cross and into her heart. "Truly I say to you, my son, this day you will be with Me in paradise."

The sky darkened and the earth shook, but Zahara's soul was filled with light. God had heard and answered the prayer she had been offering for so long. In His infinite mercy, He had reached into the heart of her rebellious son with His redemption. She would see Daniel again, but this time their hearts would be united in love and peace in the presence of God.

Through her tears, she whispered the prayer Jesus had taught them, "Our Father which art in heaven, hallowed be thy name. . . ."

Pamela Kennedy writes short stories, articles, essays, and children's books. She currently resides in Honolulu, Hawaii, with her husband, a retired naval officer. They have three adult children.

Original artwork by Doris Ettlinger.

HE IS RISEN

Cecile Frances Alexander

He is risen, He is risen;
    Tell it out with joyful voice:
He has burst His three-days' prison;
    Let the whole wide earth rejoice.
Death is conquered, man is free,
Christ has won the victory.

Come ye sad and fearful-hearted,
    With glad smile and radiant brow.
Lent's long shadows have departed.
    All His woes are over now
And the passion that He bore:
Sin and pain can vex no more.

Come with high and holy hymning;
    Chant our Lord's triumphant lay.
Not one darksome cloud is dimming
    Yonder glorious morning ray,
Breaking o'er the purple East,
Symbol of our Easter Feast.

A risen Christ,

the Savior lives,

With death and

sorrow left behind

RING, BELLS OF EASTER

Marian L. Moore

Ring gladly, bells of Easter;
Ring God's message over vale and hill
That Christ is risen from the dead,
His lasting promise to fulfill.

Ring gladly, bells of Easter;
Ring your song of faith for all mankind:
A risen Christ, the Savior lives,
With death and sorrow left behind.

California poppies, owl's clovers, and goldfields form a spring mosaic in Antelope Valley California Poppy Reserve in the Mojave Desert of California. Photograph by Jeff Gnass.

Above the Hills of Time

Thomas Tiplady

Above the hills of time the Cross is gleaming,
 Fair as the sun when night has turned to day;
And from it love's pure light is richly streaming,
 To cleanse the heart and banish sin away.
To this dear Cross the eyes of men are turning,
 Today as in the ages lost to sight;
And for love of Christ men's hearts are yearning,
 As shipwrecked seamen yearn for morning light.

The Cross, O Christ, Thy wondrous love revealing,
 Awakes our hearts as with the light of morn,
And pardon o'er our sinful spirits stealing,
 Tells us that we, in Thee, have been reborn.
Like echoes to sweet temple bells replying,
 Our hearts, O Lord, make answer to Thy love;
And we will love Thee with a love undying,
 Till we are gathered to Thy home above.

A prairie on Cascade Head, above the mouth of the Salmon River and the Oregon headlands, is dotted with hairy-stemmed checker-mallows. Photograph by Terry Donnelly/Donnelly Austin Photography.

DEVOTIONS FROM THE HEART

Pamela Kennedy

On the evening of that first day of the week, when the disciples were together with the doors locked for fear of the Jews, Jesus came and stood among them and said, "Peace be with you!" —John 20:19 (NIV)

LOCKED DOORS

"There are parts of my life I could never share with anyone," the woman said. We sat together on a couch at a retreat center. "I've caused my children so much pain. I've made poor choices. I lived my life the way I wanted. And now I have to deal with the consequences."

"Don't you believe they would forgive you if you told them how you feel?" I asked.

"I don't think I deserve forgiveness. Not from them and certainly not from God. Besides, I'm afraid. What if I did take the risk of asking to be forgiven and were refused? I'm not sure I could take that rejection." She dabbed at her eyes with a piece of well-used tissue and sighed heavily.

I wanted to comfort her, to encourage her, but what could I say to ease her pain and relieve her fears? She had decided to lock the doors of her heart, to keep her pain inside and everyone else locked out. She gathered her things and apologized for burdening me with her concerns. I assured her it was no burden, but I felt inadequate. Didn't I sometimes lock the door to my heart too? Weren't there situations where I refused to let out my pain, to share a deep heartache, or to let someone else comfort me?

It was a few days later, in re-reading the account of the first Easter written by the Apostle John, that I found a key to reaching my hurting friend and a key to my own locked heart as well.

It was late on that first Resurrection Day. Earlier, the disciples had heard Mary Magdalene's account of finding the stone rolled away from the tomb where Jesus had been buried. To check out

---

Dear Heavenly Father, forgive me for the times I try to lock You and others out of my heart. When I am afraid, please give me the courage to invite You in and accept Your peace. Amen.

---

her story, Peter and John dashed to the tomb; they found only the empty burial clothes. Jesus was gone, but they had no idea what had happened to His body. Perplexed, they returned to their homes; but Mary stayed outside the tomb weeping. Then, turning to leave, she encountered a man she assumed to be the gardener. When He spoke her name, however, she recognized Him as the risen Lord. He urged her to run and tell the others that

Photograph by Jessie Walker.

He was alive and that He would soon return to God. Mary hurried to share the good news.

By that evening, the disciples were gathered together in a small room with the door locked. They were afraid. The Scriptures say they feared the Jews, but they were probably also afraid for God to find them out. They had acted as cowards, deserting their Lord in His hour of need. A few days earlier they had run from the soldiers who came to arrest Jesus, and Peter had even denied that he knew Him. They were locked away with their shame and fear, longing only to be left alone.

Then Jesus came and stood among them. Unhindered by the locked door, the darkness, or their fear, He just appeared. And His words were not ones of condemnation or disappointment, but of love. "Peace be with you!" He said. And I can imagine their hearts leaping for joy.

These were the very words my friend needed to hear. She needed to know that her locked door could not keep out God's love because He wanted to give her peace in place of her fears and guilt.

I quickly wrote her a note, telling her what I had discovered. Before sealing the envelope, I slipped in a tiny silver key. I hoped it would remind her that though we may try to lock Him out, God always finds a way to open the door and offer us peace.

To the Easter Lilies

Helen Elizabeth Williamson

Beneath the winter soil you sit
As servants in your humble tents,
Till urgings, ah, benevolent,
Uplift you from earth's somber pit
To bathe in warm spring days sunlit—
Your guileless blooms magnificent,
Their robes of white a testament
Of loveliness that's infinite.

Stately lilies, flower apostles,
On Easter morn your trumpets ring
With perfumed breath as they exhale,
"The Lord is risen! Dance and sing."
Lift our hearts with peals colossal.
Hallelujah! Life prevails.

Resurrection

Emily May Young

The promise of resurrection
Is not only told in the Book;
It is heralded in the springtime
By every happy brook.

It is announced by violets
And by the dogwood trees.
It is chanted by the mockingbird
And the buzz of myriad bees.

It is echoed every Easter
By the lily's perfumed breath,
When every sleeping plant awakes,
Triumphant over death.

The white Easter lily is one of the loveliest of nature's spring display.
Photograph by A. Teufen/H. Armstrong Roberts.

Flower Carol

Translated from the Latin

Spring has now unwrapped the flowers;
    Day is fast reviving;
Life in all her growing powers
    Towards the light is striving.
Gone the iron touch of cold,
    Wintertime and frost time;
Seedlings, working through the mold,
    Now make up for lost time.

Herb and plant that, winter long,
    Slumbered at their leisure,
Now bestirring, green and strong,
    Find in growth their pleasure.
All the world with beauty fills,
    Gold the green enhancing;
Flowers make glee among the hills
    And set the meadows dancing.

Through each wonder of fair days
    God Himself expresses;
Beauty follows all His ways,
    As the world He blesses.
So as He renews the earth,
    Artist without rival,
In His grace of glad new birth
    We must seek revival.

Earth puts on her dress of glee;
    Flowers and grasses hide her;
We go forth in charity—
    Brothers all beside her;
For, as man this glory sees
    In the awakening season,
Reason learns the heart's decrees,
    And hearts are led by reason.

Praise the Maker, all ye saints;
    He with glory girt you;
He who skies and meadows paints
    Fashioned all your virtue;
Praise Him, seers, heroes, kings,
    Heralds of perfection;
Brothers, praise Him, for He brings
    All to Resurrection!

Delicate shades of pink rhododendrons and rich purple and blush tulips, with the soft touch of yellow daffodils, make this garden lovely. Photograph by Mary Liz Austin/Donnelly Austin Photography.

READERS' FORUM

Snapshots from IDEALS readers

Right: Three-year-old Sarah Margaret Soden, daughter of Gary and Antoinette Soden, loves her new pink raincoat and umbrella so much that she likes to wear them even on sunny days, according to her grandmother, Margaret Soden of Pompton Plains, New Jersey.

Left: Bluebonnets and Indian paintbrushes have bloomed just in time to tickle the nose of Brylie Suzanne Leach, daughter of Robert and Donna Leach of Savoy, Texas. This snapshot is shared with IDEALS readers by Great-grandmother Gladys Stone.

Below left: "So this happens every spring?" Nathan Robert McCormick is fascinated by early daffodils in his grandmother's garden. He is the nine-month-old grandson of Margaret Humphrey of Adamsville, Alabama, and the son of Greg and Ellen McCormick of Portage, Michigan.

Top: Gabrielle Elisa Grace is the loveliest flower in the meadow by her church. She is the twenty-one-month-old daughter of Kevin and Jennifer Grace of Ballston Lake, New York.

Right: A delicate touch . . . Michaela Lynn Slaughter, granddaughter of Sharon Slaughter, of Cobbs Creek, Virginia, gently holds her spring discovery. Her grandmother reports that the nineteen-month-old chose to play with the flowers over her pink ball.

Below: "You're never too young to start reading IDEALS," says Joan Richards of Chagrin Falls, Ohio, proud grandmother of Collin Bell, ten months old. Collin is the son of Ken and Julie Bell.

Dear Reader,

On Easter mornings, Mother would wake me while it was still dark and chilly outside. I would dress, groggy and stiff in the cold, in a sweater and a warm skirt with flat-heeled pumps. Breakfast would be hours later.

Just before dawn, we would meet the rest of the community choir on the campus of Castle Heights Military Academy. We would hastily don the choir robes from our individual churches. Ours from the First Baptist Church were cream-colored; others were maroon or blue. We would hurriedly find our places and form graduated rows on the steps of Macfadden Auditorium. As soon as the first light of the sun touched the tops of the oak trees lining the drive, the director raised his arms and led us in an a capella version of the "Hallelujah Chorus" from Handel's *The Messiah.*

On the occasion of my mother's funeral, the members of that community choir came together once more with the same director and again sang the "Hallelujah Chorus." The resounding words of Revelation gave comfort then, as they have for centuries: *"The kingdoms of this world are become the kingdoms of our Lord, and of his Christ; and he shall reign for ever and ever"* (11:15).

Publisher, Patricia A. Pingry
Editor, Marjorie L. Lloyd
Designer, Royce DeGrie
Copy Editor, Melinda Rathjen
Permissions Editor, Patsy Jay
Contributing Writers, Lansing Christman, Joan Donaldson, Pamela Kennedy, Teresa Schell, Brenda Wilt, and Lois Winston

ACKNOWLEDGMENTS

GUEST, EDGAR A. "April" from *The George Matthew Adams Service,* 1961. Used by permission of M. Henry Sobell, III. JAQUES, EDNA "Spring" from *The Golden Road* by Edna Jaques, published by Thomas Allen, Ltd., © 1953. Used by permission of Louise Bonnell. MOORE, LILIAN. "Forsythia Bush" from *I Thought I Heard the City* by Lilian Moore. Copyright © 1969 by Lilian Moore, renewed © 1997 by Lilian Moore Reavin. Used by permission of Marian Reiner. STRONG, PATIENCE. "The Prophecy" from *Where Memory Leads* by Patience Strong, published by Muller, 1951. Used by permission of Rupert Crew Ltd. TIPLADY, THOMAS. "Above the Hills of Time." Used by permission of Hope Publishing Company. Our sincere thanks to those those authors, or their heirs, who submitted poems or articles to IDEALS for publication. Every possible effort has been made to acknowledge ownership of material used.

Inside back cover: Spring daffodils seem to burst from the formal confines of this blue ceramic vase in this painting entitled STILL LIFE OF SPRING FLOWERS by Louis John Rhead (1857–1926). Image from Fine Art Photographic Library, Ltd., London/Angela Hone Watercolours.

STATEMENT OF OWNERSHIP, MANAGEMENT AND CIRCULATION (REQUIRED BY FORM 3526)

1. Publication Title: Ideals. 2. Publication Number: 0019-137X. 3. Filing Date: August 11, 2005. 4. Issue Frequency: Bi-Monthly. 5. Number of Issues Published Annually: 6. 6. Annual Subscription Price: $19.95. 7. Office of publication: Guideposts a Church Corporation, 39 Seminary Hill Road, Carmel, NY 10512. 8. Location of headquarters: Guideposts a Church Corporation, 39 Seminary Hill Road, Carmel, NY 10512. 9. The names and addresses of the publisher and the editor-in-chief are: Patricia A. Pingry, Ideals Publications, A Division of Guideposts, 535 Metroplex Dr., Ste. 250, Nashville, TN 37211; Editor: Marjorie L. Lloyd (same as publisher). 10. Owner: Guideposts a Church Corporation, a New York not for-profit corporation, 39 Seminary Hill Road, Carmel, NY 10512. Names and addresses of individual owners; None. 11. The known bondholders, mortgagees, and other security holders owning or holding one percent or more of total amount of bonds, mortgages or other securities: None. 12. The exempt status has not changed during preceding 12 months. 13. Publication Name: Ideals. 14. Issue Date for Circulation Data: August 5, 2005. 15. Average number of copies each issue during preceding twelve months: a. total number of copies printed: 143,321; b. (1) paid and/or requested circulation through outside-county mail subscriptions: 106,247; (2) paid and/or requested circulation through in-county subscriptions: None; (3) paid and/or requested circulation through dealer sales: 18,952; (4) paid and/or requested circulation through other classes: None; c. total paid and/or requested circulation: 125,200. d. (1) free distribution by mail through outside county: 833; (2) free distribution by mail through in-county: None; (3) free distribution by mail through other classes: None; e. free distribution outside the mail: 4,979; f. total free distribution: 5,813; g. total distribution: 131,012; h. copies not distributed: 12,308; i. total: 143,321. Percent Paid and/or requested circulation: 95.6%. Actual number of copies of single issue published nearest to filing date: 15.a. total number of copies printed: 126,983; b. (1) paid and/or requested circulation through outside-county mail subscriptions: 114,336; (2) paid and/or requested circulation through in-county subscriptions: None; (3) paid and/or requested circulation through dealer sales: 2,698; (4) paid and/or requested circulation through other classes: None; c. total paid and/or requested circulation: 117,034; d. (1) free distribution by mail through outside-county: 1,000; (2) free distribution by mail through in-county: None; (3) free distribution by mail through other classes: None; e. free distribution outside the mail: None; f. total free distribution: 1,000; g. total distribution: 118,034; h. copies not distributed: 8,949; i. total: 126,983. Percent Paid and/or requested circulation: 99.2%. 16. This Statement of Ownership will be printed in the Easter '06 issue of this publication. 17. I certify that the statements made to me above are correct and complete.

Signed, John F. Temple, President